For Maureen, Sean & Steph,
and for Andrea, too
J. L.

For Jaz
M. T.

I would like to thank Dr. Rebecca Lewison, hippo expert,
for reading my text and making invaluable comments.

Text copyright © 2015 by Jonathan London
Illustrations copyright © 2015 by Matthew Trueman

First edition 2015

Library of Congress Catalog Card Number 2014944797
ISBN 978-0-7636-6592-0

14 15 16 17 18 19 CCP 10 9 8 7 6 5 4 3 2 1

Printed in Shenzhen, Guangdong, China

This book was typeset in Badger and Agenda.
The illustrations were done in mixed media.

Candlewick Press
99 Dover Street
Somerville, Massachusetts 02144

visit us at www.candlewick.com

HIPPOS ARE HUGE!

Jonathan London

illustrated by **Matthew Trueman**

CANDLEWICK PRESS

Hippos are
HUGE!
Except for elephants,
no other land animals are
as large as hippopotamuses.
They can weigh as much
as fifty men!

A full-grown bull weighs up to
4 tons and can be 12 feet
(almost 4 meters) long.

7

A hippo has the biggest mouth
of any animal except for a whale!

In fact, whales—along with
dolphins and porpoises—are
hippos' closest living relatives.

A hippo's jaws can open 4 feet (more than 1 meter). You wouldn't want to try it, but you could stand a baseball bat straight up inside a hippo's mouth.

Watch out!
Hippo's "yawn" is a threat!
It means
Stay Away!

**Which do you think is the most dangerous animal in Africa?
A lion? A crocodile?**

No!

Would you believe that the hippo is the most dangerous animal in Africa?

Though it's hard to prove, many sources claim that hippos kill more people in Africa than any other wild animal does. Mothers sometimes kill to protect their young, while bulls kill to protect their territory.

With their **monstrous** jaws and **razor-sharp** tusks, hippos can bite a giant crocodile in half or chomp a small boat in two.

And they are **fast!** They can run faster than a human and they can travel faster in water, too!

Hippos' tusks can probably grow longer than your arms!

Hippos don't really swim. **LOOK!** First Hippo dives, with her ears pressed against her head and her nostrils closed.

A hippo can run 25 miles (40 kilometers) per hour and travel 6 miles (10 kilometers) per hour in the water — faster than an Olympic swimmer! You might think such huge creatures would be awkward underwater, but they're surprisingly graceful.

12

Next, she bounces gracefully along the bottom, kicking off with her hind legs, and

gliiiiiiides . . . .

then dances on her tiptoes and kicks off again.

Like whales, hippos communicate underwater with clicks, squeaks, and deep, thunderous bellows. Hippos can hold their breath for up to five minutes.

Hippo **bursts** through the surface, spouting fountains of water from her nostrils.

Hippos must stay in water as much as possible to keep their skin from drying out. On land, their skin oozes a slimy reddish oil that acts as a sunscreen. To avoid the hot sun, hippos do their grazing at night.

When Hippo isn't dancing along in the water or chasing crocodiles, she spends most of the day with just her eyes, ears, and nose sticking out of the water, resting and watching.

A cattle egret picks its dinner of insects from Hippo's ear. A fish nips tidbits of food stuck between Hippo's teeth. **Yum!**

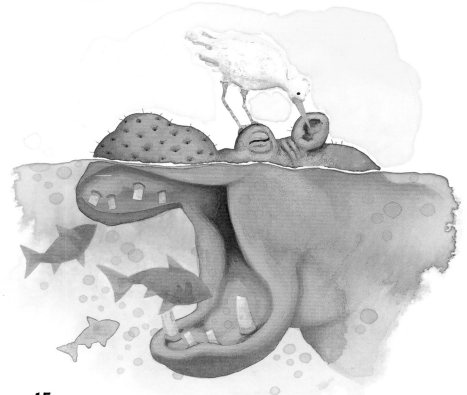

You might think that hippos would snap at birds or fish that came near them, but they don't — because they're helping each other.

Just then, a great commotion erupts!
And Hippo watches as two bulls
square off.

The two bulls turn
and stand rump to rump.
Then they swing their tails
like baseball bats and
swat balls of dung
at each other—

A male hippo is called a bull,
a female is called a cow, and
a baby is called a calf.

SP
SP

LAT!
LOP!

It's a
smelly message
to
KEEP OUT!

When this doesn't work, the defending bull "yawns" to show off his powerful tusks . . . then pounces with a great

ROAAAAAA

Battles can be bloody and can rage for more than an hour. Both bulls will show battle scars.

AAAR! and attacks with giant jaws.

Hippo watches as they **honk** and **snort. . .** until, finally, the defeated bull limps away.

Stronger bulls get to mate with the cows in and around the nursery, where mothers take turns watching the calves. Cows start having babies when they are seven or eight years old.

In the nearby nursery,
Hippo watches baby
hippos playing.

Playing is good practice
for when the bulls will need to protect
their territory from other bulls.

20

Two calves play-fight in a hippo tug-of-war
with their jaws locked together.

Soon it will be Hippo's turn to mate, and in
a few months she'll have a baby of her own.

Hippos mate in shallow water, during the dry season,
and calves are born in the water eight months later,
in the rainy season, when the grass is plentiful.

Months pass. The rains come
and fill the lakes and rivers.
And now it is time.

Hippo stands
neck-deep in water,
and . . .
a baby is born!

A newborn calf weighs
100 pounds (45 kilograms)!

For the first four months, he'll only drink his mother's milk. Hippos are herbivores, and their main food is grass, which they eat at night. Adults may eat up to 100 pounds (45 kilograms) per day.

Baby Hippo paddles to the surface, and his head **pops** up for his first breath.

Then he dives back down and nudges Hippo's teats for her milk.

23

A few weeks later, Hippo and her calf
join the nursery and wallow in the mud.

They snuggle together and
gently lick and nuzzle
each other.

All hippos love to wallow in mud,
which keeps them cool.
And though hippos are ferocious,
they can be gentle, too.

Though Baby Hippo looks tiny next to
his mother, when he's six months old,
he will weigh 500 pounds!

HIPPOS ARE HUGE!

INDEX

Look up the pages to find out about all these hippopotamus things. Don't forget to look at both kinds of words — **this kind** *and* this kind.

About Hippopotamuses

Historically, hippos have lived throughout sub-Saharan Africa, but now their numbers have been vastly reduced, and they're largely confined to protected areas. In 2006, hippos were added to the Endangered Species List as "vulnerable." Still, they are hunted illegally for their meat and their ivory tusks. With help from conservationists, long may these giants who dance underwater — with their whale-size jaws and small, twirling ears — survive.